Doodle Paris

Published in 2013 by Dog 'n' Bone Books
An imprint of Ryland Peters & Small Ltd

20–21 Jockey's Fields
London WC1R 4BW

519 Broadway, 5th Floor
New York, NY 10012

www.dogandbonebooks.com

10 9 8 7 6 5 4 3 2 1

A CIP catalog record for this book is available from
the Library of Congress and the British Library.

ISBN: 978 1 909313 01 9

Printed in China

Editor: Pete Jorgensen
Design concept: Teo Connor at No Days Off
Spread design: Alison Fenton
Illustration: Rob Merrett

For digital editions, visit
www.cicobooks.com/apps.php

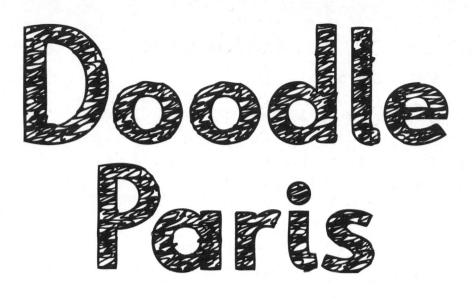

Doodle Paris

Doodle a day in one of the world's greatest cities

ROB MERRETT

DOG 'n' BONE

Introduction

Bonjour mes amis!

What is Paris? Paris is a city for all the senses. It's a city for lovers, for artists, for fabulous food and fashion.
A place to discover museums and art galleries, exquisite parks, flamboyant statues, breathtaking monuments, and grand architecture.

For a foreign city, it somehow seems oddly familiar to the stranger. Maybe that's because it appears so often in history, film, magazines, and television.

There may indeed be delightful pâtisseries, florists, perfumeries, fashion boutiques, and junk shops in other major cities around the world, but in Paris, they are absolutely DIVINE! They seem to have more color, more imagination, more drama, more luxury…in fact, they just have MORE!

Maybe it's just me, but there is a frisson of excitement and delightful sense of impending discovery every time I wander through the quaint lanes of the Marias—a Paris quarter steeped in history—and stroll around the fascinating open-air food markets, walk across the impressive courtyard of the Louvre, or cross the Seine by the most beautiful bridge in Paris, Pont Alexandre III.

Paris is a jewel like no other and that's why it's often referred to as 'The City of Light.' It sparkles, just like the Eiffel tower that twinkles at night every hour, on the hour.

"I love Paris in the springtime.
I love Paris in the fall.
I love Paris in the summer when it sizzles.
I love Paris in the winter when it drizzles."

Cole Porter, American composer and songwriter

My sentiments exactly!

This doodle book offers you a fun, informative, and eclectic tour of Paris, traveling at break-neck speed with over 100 pages of delightful sketches to complete or create from scratch. There is everything from simple join-the-dots puzzles and adding figures to an everyday Paris scene to designing fashion accessories and concocting mouth-watering culinary delights. If you know Paris well, draw what you remember from your visits. If you've never been, this doodle book is guaranteed to whet your appetite for Paris and will encourage your imagination to run freely through the grand avenues, elegant squares, glamorous fashion boutiques, and charming green spaces of this thrilling city!

Bon voyage!

Carte Postale

Correspondance

Adresse

Reflect the Eiffel Tower in the waters of the Seine.

What are the customers at this café having for breakfast?

Draw chic Parisiennes walking in the Tuileries Garden.

How many French tarts do you know? Draw their fillings.

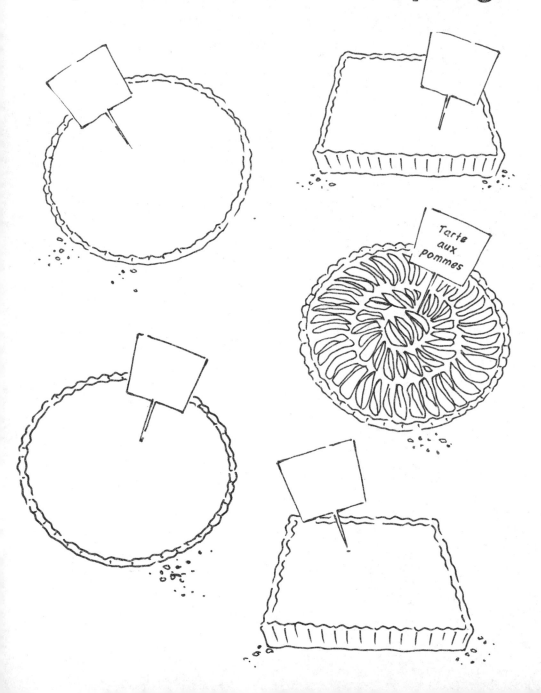

Tarte
aux
pommes

Give these can-can dancers boldly patterned stockings.

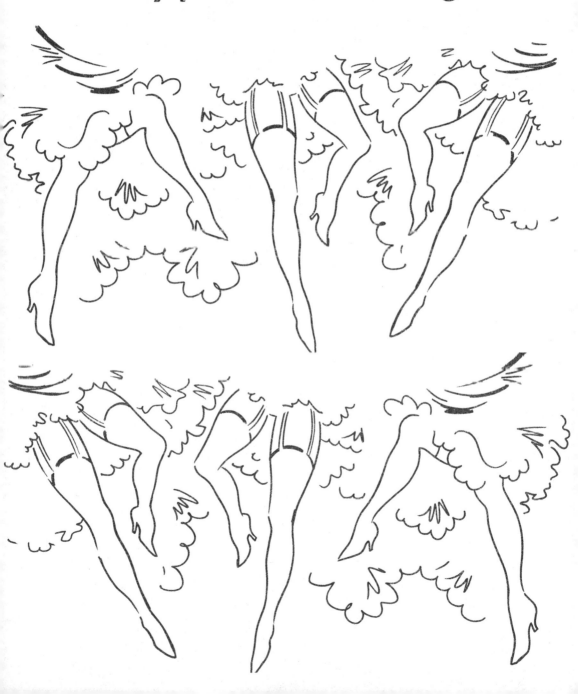

Join the dots to discover the most famous landmark in Paris.

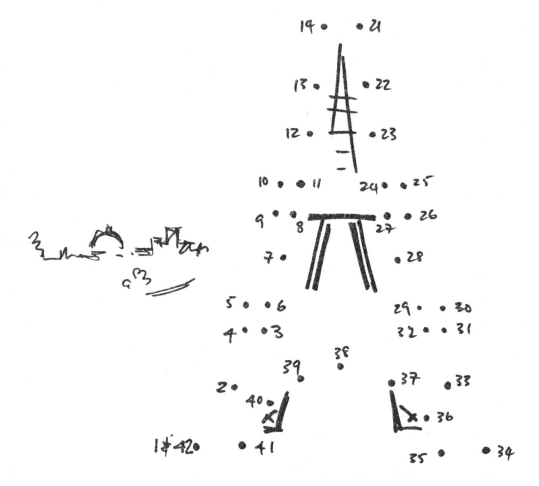

Draw your favorite French dish.

This gargoyle looks really lonely.

Draw him some friends.

What type of boutique is this?
Dress the windows s'il vous plaît.

BOUTIQUE

Decorate the Arc de Triomphe.
What will you put on the top?

Who is standing on the Pont Neuf?

What are they looking at on the Seine?

Join the dots to reveal one really scary Parisian.

Decorate these Parisian shopping bags.

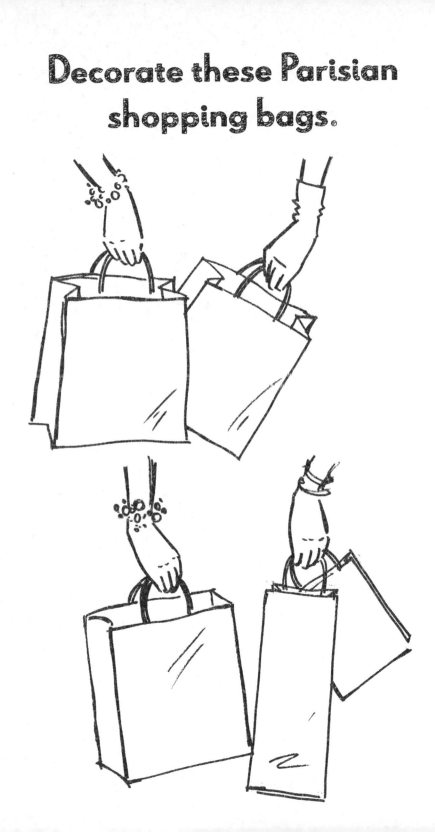

Join the dots to discover the number one nibble in Paris.

Draw your favorite French dessert... yum!

What mouth-watering delicacies are in this box?

Identify these delicious treats from the pâtisserie.

éclair

c   b

m

p

c

c

b

financier

r

t   c

p   f

canelé

Vive la baguette!

Create your perfect lunchtime snack.

It's Christmas in Place Vendôme. Add festive cheer to the column.

Fill this snow globe with your favorite Paris landmarks.

Join the dots to discover what stands in Napoléon's Courtyard of the Palais du Louvre.

Draw an Eiffel-Tower inspired...

space rocket

racing car

Design an Eiffel-Tower inspired stand for this lamp.

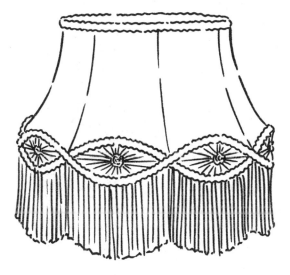

Create a chic Parisian pattern for the shade.

It's time to hit the town.
Draw Eiffel-Tower inspired...

earrings for your ears

and heels for your shoes.

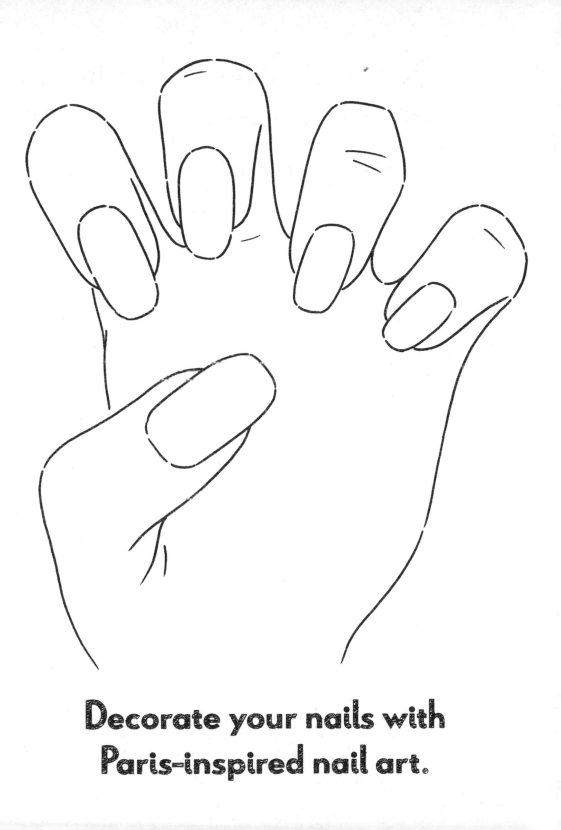

Decorate your nails with
Paris-inspired nail art.

Queen of France, Marie Antoinette loved big hair. Create a new style for her.

Join the dots to discover one of the most popular pets in Paris.

You've moved to Paris!

Furnish your apartment in style!

Marie Antoinette has lost her head. Give her a new one.

Draw a line of can-can dancers outside the Moulin Rouge.

Give these French bulldogs their missing black patches.

Why not try polka dots or stripes!

Draw some more delicious hors d'oeuvre to serve at a cocktail party.

The Café de Flore is famous for its fashionable clientele.

Draw them sitting outside.

Write a postcard to your best friend.

Anyone for escargot?

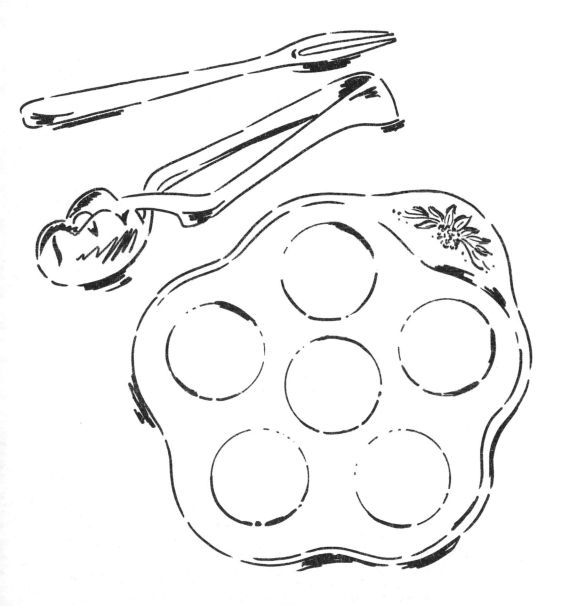

Fill this plate with snails.

It's Couture Fashion Week in Paris...

draw your favorite outfits.

Dress Edith Piaf in a fabulous couture gown.

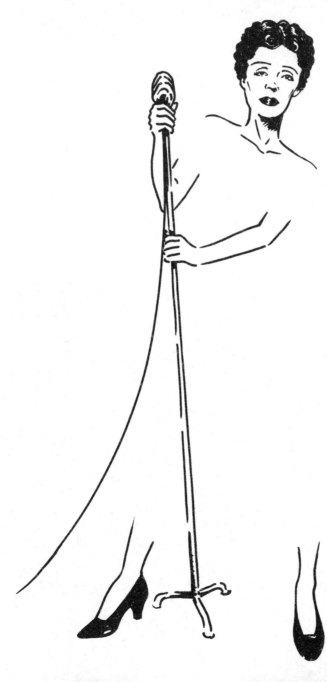

Aujourd'hui

What's on the menu today?

Draw a sky full of parachute jumpers.

Fill this chic salon with poodles.

Hold a cocktail party for your Parisian friends.

Saint-Germain is packed with quaint boutiques and hotels.

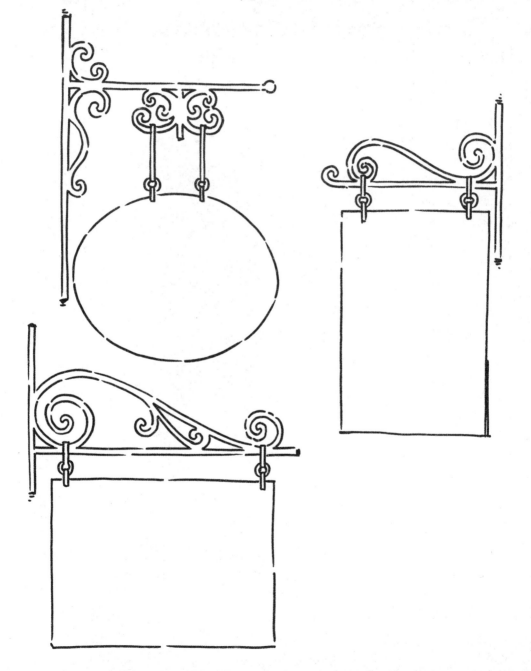

Design their signs.

Fill this Batobus with Parisian commuters.

Draw some antiques that have caught your eye.

ANTIQUITES

Paris is for lovers,
draw a romantic couple.

Create a traffic jam around the Arc de Triomphe.

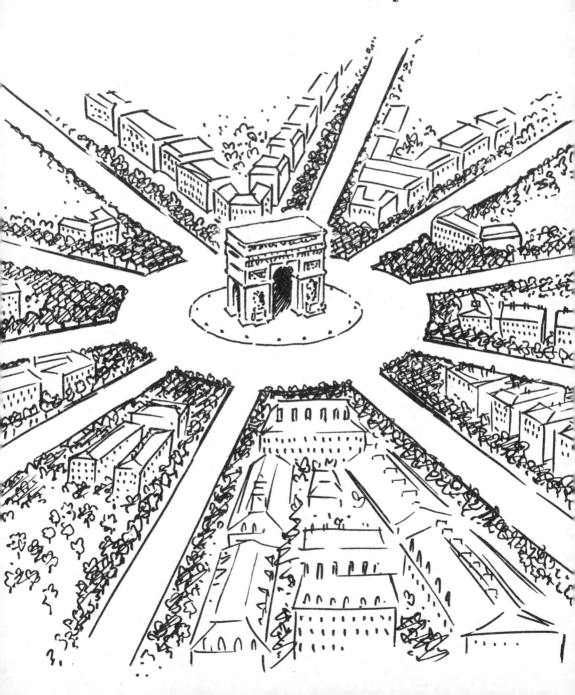

CHAPEAUX

Which hats would you like to try on?
Draw the vendeuse at the door.

Give these Parisian pooches...

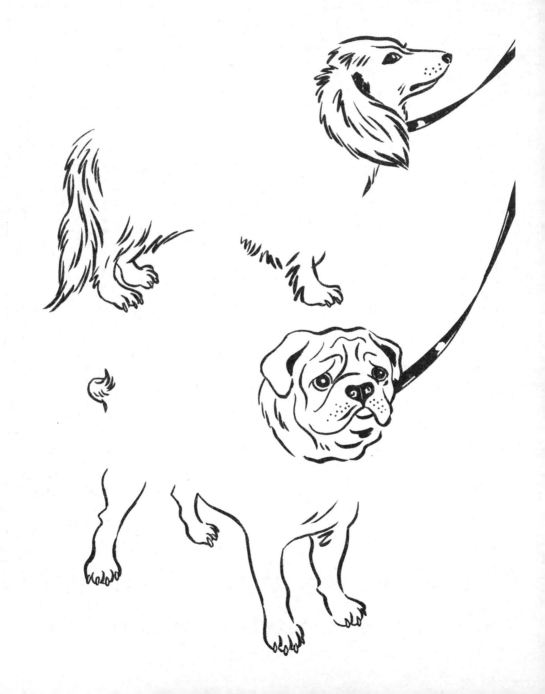

chic cold-weather cover-ups.

Who is taking the Metro?

You've discovered the most beautiful flower shop in Paris!

What flowers do they sell?

Cover the dome of Sacré-Coeur
with flowers or polka dots.

This Parisian tipple comes in a floral bottle. Design your own.

It's Summer in Paris.

Draw some must-have sunglasses.

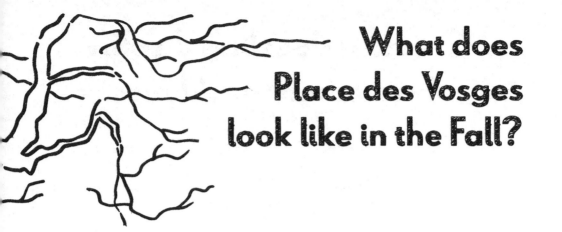

What does Place des Vosges look like in the Fall?

Create a dazzling display of statement necklaces.

BIJOUX FANTAISIE

Coiffeur Antoine

Draw Monsieur Antoine at work on a VIP client.

Decorate these umbrellas...

to brighten a rainy day in Paris.

Draw the four things you'd like to see most on the balcony of your Paris apartment.

Parisian haute CAT - ure!

Dress these fashionable felines.

Give this gent a beret, baguette, wine bottle, and striped T-shirt.

Fill the shop windows with divine bags and shoes.

AU JOYEUX
MOULIN ROUGE

SPECTACLE · CONCERT · BAL

Design a poster for the
Moulin Rouge.

Add the hieroglyphics missing from the obelisk in Place de la Concorde.

Add skulls and bones missing from the spooky Paris catacombs.

The final stage of the Tour de France
ends on the Champs Élysées.

Is this rider in the lead or is he way behind?

Create a charming
winter hat, perhaps in the
shape of a croissant!

What has this Parisian street artist drawn on the pavement?

Parisians celebrate Bastille Day with fireworks. Draw an amazing display.

What is displayed on this bookseller's stall?

Summer has arrived in Paris! Fill the temporary beach along the Seine with sun worshippers.

Napoléon and Josephine are moving to the Left Bank.

What is Josephine taking with her?

Pampered Parisian pets are always carried in handbags.

Create some of your own designs.

Who is on stage tonight...

at the Opera Palais Garnier?

Create two masterworks...

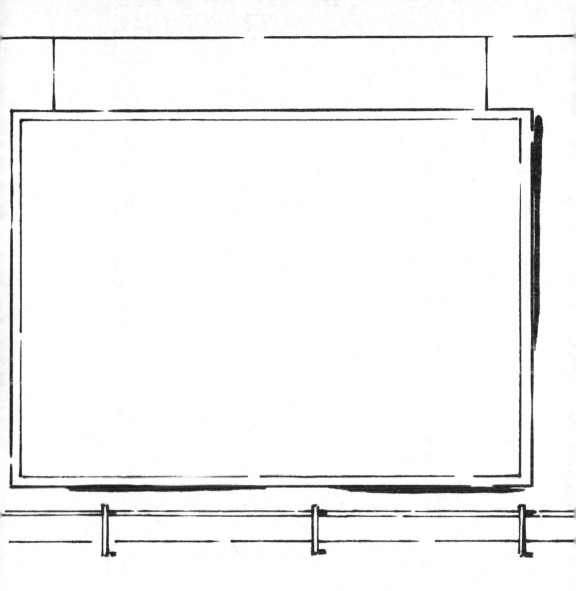

to hang in the Louvre.

What is reflected in the mirror?

Fill these shelves with fabulous French fragrances.

The Louvre is home to this famous lady.

Give her a modern make-over.

The famous exterior of the Pompidou Center has been renovated. How does it look now?

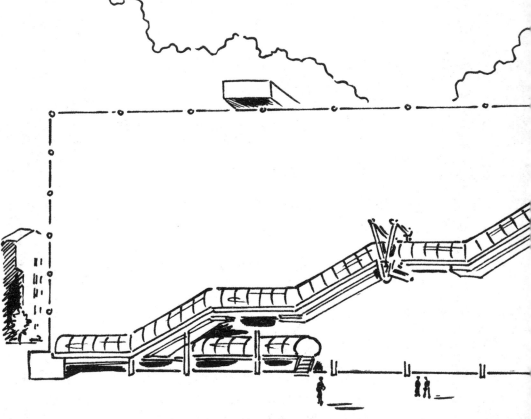

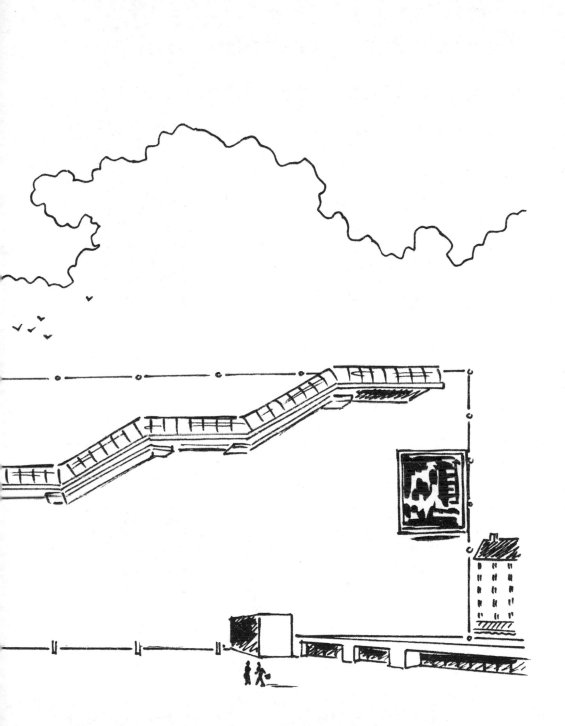

Add shutters, railings, and flower boxes to these apartment windows.

Give these ancient marble
statues "I Love Paris" T-shirts.

Give these crêpes sweet and savory fillings.

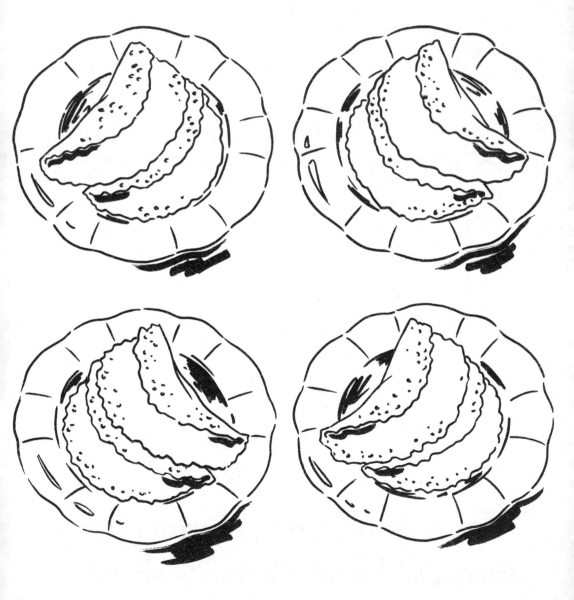

An artist in Montmatre is drawing your portrait. What do you and the sketch look like?

Berthillon has the best
ice cream in Paris!
Create three delicious sundaes.

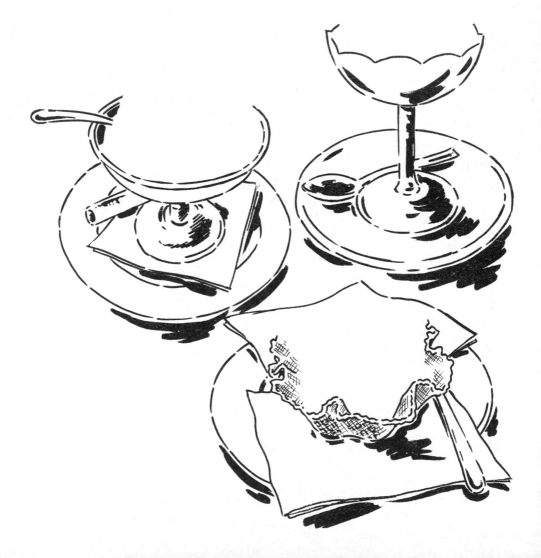

Visit the Sunday bird market on Ile de la Cité.

Which birds are for sale?

The fashion cognoscenti are in
Paris for the haute-couture shows.

Draw you and your best friends in the front row.

Parisians like to indulge in a spot of topiary.

Style some of your own plants into interesting shapes.

Who is taking baby for a stroll ...

in the Jardin du Luxembourg?

It's fashion show time again!

Give these front row spectators some serious heels.

Create a delightful spring hat
with ribbons, feathers, and
famous Paris landmarks.

Fill these bags with groceries. Include bread, cheese, and wine.

Draw the rooftops of Paris.